VIVIAN TENORIO

HIGH SCHOOL JOURNAL

This journal belongs to:

_____

VIVIAN TENORIO

HIGH SCHOOL JOURNAL
4-YEAR JOURNAL OF MY HIGH SCHOOL YEARS

BY VIVIAN TENORIO

JAV PUBLISHING

Printed in the United Stated of America

www.viviantenorio.com

ISBN-10: 1530764947
ISBN-13: 978-1530764945

"The future belongs to those who believe in the beauty of their dreams." -Eleanor Roosevelt

Other Books by Vivian Tenorio:

Pink Slip to Product Launch in a Weak Economy

Pregnancy Journal: heartwarming memories

High School Journal: 4-year journal of my high school years

Wisdom Journal: wisdom worth passing on

Dating Journal: remember why you fell in love

2012 - 2019 Gratitude Journal: magical moments should be remembered forever

2012 - 2019 Dream Journal: remember your dreams forever

In Spanish

Diario de Embarazo: tiernos recuerdos

2012 – 2016 Diario de Gratitud: los momentos mágicos deben ser recordados

2012 – 2016 Diario de Sueños: recuerde sus suenos para siempre

About me … Freshman Year

FAVORITE COLOR:
LUCKY NUMBER:
HOBBIES:
BOYFRIEND:
FAVORITE DESSERT:
FAVORITE TEACHER:
FAVORITE BOOK:
WHERE DO YOU WORK:
FAVORITE TV SHOW:

LOOKING FORWARD TO WHAT THIS YEAR:

About me … Sophomore Year

FAVORITE COLOR:
LUCKY NUMBER:
HOBBIES:
BOYFRIEND:
FAVORITE DESSERT:
FAVORITE TEACHER:
FAVORITE BOOK:
WHERE DO YOU WORK:
FAVORITE TV SHOW:

LOOKING FORWARD TO WHAT THIS YEAR:

About me ... Junior Year

FAVORITE COLOR:

LUCKY NUMBER:

HOBBIES:

BOYFRIEND:

FAVORITE DESSERT:

FAVORITE TEACHER:

FAVORITE BOOK:

WHERE DO YOU WORK:

FAVORITE TV SHOW:

LOOKING FORWARD TO WHAT THIS YEAR:

About me ... Senior Year

FAVORITE COLOR:

LUCKY NUMBER:

HOBBIES:

BOYFRIEND:

FAVORITE DESSERT:

FAVORITE TEACHER:

FAVORITE BOOK:

WHERE DO YOU WORK:

FAVORITE TV SHOW:

LOOKING FORWARD TO WHAT THIS YEAR:

Freshman Picture

PLACE PICTURE
HERE

DATE   /   /   LOVE?   ☐ Yes   ☐ No

VIVIAN TENORIO

DATE   /   / 20   freshman

DATE   /   / 20   sophomore

DATE   /   / 20   junior

DATE   /   / 20   senior

DATE   /   / 20   freshman

DATE   /   / 20   sophomore

DATE   /   / 20   junior

DATE   /   / 20   senior

VIVIAN TENORIO

DATE   /   / 20   freshman

DATE   /   / 20   sophomore

DATE   /   / 20   junior

DATE   /   / 20   senior

DATE   /   / 20   freshman

DATE   /   / 20   sophomore

DATE   /   / 20   junior

DATE   /   / 20   senior

VIVIAN TENORIO

DATE ___/___/ 20____   freshman

DATE ___/___/ 20____   sophomore

DATE ___/___/ 20____   junior

DATE ___/___/ 20____   senior

HIGH SCHOOL JOURNAL

DATE   /   / 20   freshman

DATE   /   / 20   sophomore

DATE   /   / 20   junior

DATE   /   / 20   senior

DATE   /   / 20   freshman

DATE   /   / 20   sophomore

DATE   /   / 20   junior

DATE   /   / 20   senior

DATE   /   / 20   freshman

DATE   /   / 20   sophomore

DATE   /   / 20   junior

DATE   /   / 20   senior

VIVIAN TENORIO

DATE   /   / 20   freshman

DATE   /   / 20   sophomore

DATE   /   / 20   junior

DATE   /   / 20   senior

DATE   /   / 20   freshman

DATE   /   / 20   sophomore

DATE   /   / 20   junior

DATE   /   / 20   senior

DATE   /   / 20   freshman

DATE   /   / 20   sophomore

DATE   /   / 20   junior

DATE   /   / 20   senior

DATE   /   / 20   freshman

DATE   /   / 20   sophomore

DATE   /   / 20   junior

DATE   /   / 20   senior

VIVIAN TENORIO

DATE   /   / 20   freshman

DATE   /   / 20   sophomore

DATE   /   / 20   junior

DATE   /   / 20   senior

DATE   /   / 20   freshman

DATE   /   / 20   sophomore

DATE   /   / 20   junior

DATE   /   / 20   senior

VIVIAN TENORIO

DATE   /   / 20   freshman

DATE   /   / 20   sophomore

DATE   /   / 20   junior

DATE   /   / 20   senior

DATE   /   / 20   freshman

DATE   /   / 20   sophomore

DATE   /   / 20   junior

DATE   /   / 20   senior

DATE   /   / 20   freshman

DATE   /   / 20   sophomore

DATE   /   / 20   junior

DATE   /   / 20   senior

DATE   /   / 20   freshman

DATE   /   / 20   sophomore

DATE   /   / 20   junior

DATE   /   / 20   senior

VIVIAN TENORIO

DATE ___ / ___ / 20 ___   freshman
_____

DATE ___ / ___ / 20 ___   sophomore
_____

DATE ___ / ___ / 20 ___   junior
_____

DATE ___ / ___ / 20 ___   senior
_____

DATE   /   / 20   freshman

DATE   /   / 20   sophomore

DATE   /   / 20   junior

DATE   /   / 20   senior

VIVIAN TENORIO

DATE   /   / 20   freshman

DATE   /   / 20   sophomore

DATE   /   / 20   junior

DATE   /   / 20   senior

SOPHMORE Picture

PLACE PICTURE
HERE

DATE   /   /   LOVE? ☐ Yes ☐ No

VIVIAN TENORIO

DATE   /   / 20   freshman

DATE   /   / 20   sophomore

DATE   /   / 20   junior

DATE   /   / 20   senior

DATE   /   / 20   freshman

DATE   /   / 20   sophomore

DATE   /   / 20   junior

DATE   /   / 20   senior

VIVIAN TENORIO

DATE   /   / 20   freshman

DATE   /   / 20   sophomore

DATE   /   / 20   junior

DATE   /   / 20   senior

DATE _____ / _____ / 20 _____   freshman

DATE _____ / _____ / 20 _____   sophomore

DATE _____ / _____ / 20 _____   junior

DATE _____ / _____ / 20 _____   senior

VIVIAN TENORIO

DATE   /   / 20   freshman

DATE   /   / 20   sophomore

DATE   /   / 20   junior

DATE   /   / 20   senior

DATE   /   / 20   freshman

DATE   /   / 20   sophomore

DATE   /   / 20   junior

DATE   /   / 20   senior

VIVIAN TENORIO

DATE   /   / 20   freshman

DATE   /   / 20   sophomore

DATE   /   / 20   junior

DATE   /   / 20   senior

DATE   /   / 20   freshman

DATE   /   / 20   sophomore

DATE   /   / 20   junior

DATE   /   / 20   senior

DATE   /   / 20   freshman

DATE   /   / 20   sophomore

DATE   /   / 20   junior

DATE   /   / 20   senior

DATE   /   / 20   freshman

DATE   /   / 20   sophomore

DATE   /   / 20   junior

DATE   /   / 20   senior

VIVIAN TENORIO

DATE   /   / 20   freshman

DATE   /   / 20   sophomore

DATE   /   / 20   junior

DATE   /   / 20   senior

DATE   /   / 20   freshman

DATE   /   / 20   sophomore

DATE   /   / 20   junior

DATE   /   / 20   senior

VIVIAN TENORIO

DATE   /   / 20   freshman

DATE   /   / 20   sophomore

DATE   /   / 20   junior

DATE   /   / 20   senior

DATE   /   / 20   freshman

DATE   /   / 20   sophomore

DATE   /   / 20   junior

DATE   /   / 20   senior

VIVIAN TENORIO

DATE   /   / 20   freshman

DATE   /   / 20   sophomore

DATE   /   / 20   junior

DATE   /   / 20   senior

DATE   /   / 20   freshman

DATE   /   / 20   sophomore

DATE   /   / 20   junior

DATE   /   / 20   senior

VIVIAN TENORIO

DATE _____ / _____ / 20 _____   freshman

DATE _____ / _____ / 20 _____   sophomore

DATE _____ / _____ / 20 _____   junior

DATE _____ / _____ / 20 _____   senior

JUNIOR Picture

PLACE PICTURE
HERE

DATE   /   /   LOVE?   ☐ Yes   ☐ No

VIVIAN TENORIO

DATE _____ / _____ / 20 _____   freshman

DATE _____ / _____ / 20 _____   sophomore

DATE _____ / _____ / 20 _____   junior

DATE _____ / _____ / 20 _____   senior

DATE   /   / 20   freshman

DATE   /   / 20   sophomore

DATE   /   / 20   junior

DATE   /   / 20   senior

DATE   /   / 20   freshman

DATE   /   / 20   sophomore

DATE   /   / 20   junior

DATE   /   / 20   senior

DATE   /   / 20   freshman

DATE   /   / 20   sophomore

DATE   /   / 20   junior

DATE   /   / 20   senior

DATE   /   / 20   freshman

DATE   /   / 20   sophomore

DATE   /   / 20   junior

DATE   /   / 20   senior

DATE   /   / 20   freshman

DATE   /   / 20   sophomore

DATE   /   / 20   junior

DATE   /   / 20   senior

VIVIAN TENORIO

DATE   /   / 20   freshman

DATE   /   / 20   sophomore

DATE   /   / 20   junior

DATE   /   / 20   senior

DATE   /   / 20   freshman

DATE   /   / 20   sophomore

DATE   /   / 20   junior

DATE   /   / 20   senior

VIVIAN TENORIO

DATE   /   / 20   freshman

DATE   /   / 20   sophomore

DATE   /   / 20   junior

DATE   /   / 20   senior

DATE   /   / 20   freshman

DATE   /   / 20   sophomore

DATE   /   / 20   junior

DATE   /   / 20   senior

VIVIAN TENORIO

DATE   /   / 20   freshman

DATE   /   / 20   sophomore

DATE   /   / 20   junior

DATE   /   / 20   senior

DATE   /   / 20   freshman

DATE   /   / 20   sophomore

DATE   /   / 20   junior

DATE   /   / 20   senior

VIVIAN TENORIO

DATE ___ / ___ / 20 ___   freshman
_____

DATE ___ / ___ / 20 ___   sophomore
_____

DATE ___ / ___ / 20 ___   junior
_____

DATE ___ / ___ / 20 ___   senior
_____

DATE   /   / 20   freshman

DATE   /   / 20   sophomore

DATE   /   / 20   junior

DATE   /   / 20   senior

VIVIAN TENORIO

SENIOR Picture

PLACE PICTURE
HERE

DATE   /   /   LOVE?   ☐ Yes   ☐ No

DATE   /   / 20   freshman

DATE   /   / 20   sophomore

DATE   /   / 20   junior

DATE   /   / 20   senior

VIVIAN TENORIO

DATE   /   / 20   freshman

DATE   /   / 20   sophomore

DATE   /   / 20   junior

DATE   /   / 20   senior

DATE _____ / _____ / 20 _____   freshman

DATE _____ / _____ / 20 _____   sophomore

DATE _____ / _____ / 20 _____   junior

DATE _____ / _____ / 20 _____   senior

VIVIAN TENORIO

DATE   /   / 20   freshman

DATE   /   / 20   sophomore

DATE   /   / 20   junior

DATE   /   / 20   senior

DATE   /   / 20   freshman

DATE   /   / 20   sophomore

DATE   /   / 20   junior

DATE   /   / 20   senior

VIVIAN TENORIO

DATE   /   / 20   freshman

DATE   /   / 20   sophomore

DATE   /   / 20   junior

DATE   /   / 20   senior

DATE _____ / _____ / 20 _____   freshman

DATE _____ / _____ / 20 _____   sophomore

DATE _____ / _____ / 20 _____   junior

DATE _____ / _____ / 20 _____   senior

VIVIAN TENORIO

DATE   /   / 20   freshman

DATE   /   / 20   sophomoro

DATE   /   / 20   junior

DATE   /   / 20   senior

DATE   /   / 20   freshman

DATE   /   / 20   sophomore

DATE   /   / 20   junior

DATE   /   / 20   senior

VIVIAN TENORIO

DATE   /   / 20   freshman

DATE   /   / 20   sophomore

DATE   /   / 20   junior

DATE   /   / 20   senior

DATE _____ / _____ / 20 _____   freshman

DATE _____ / _____ / 20 _____   sophomore

DATE _____ / _____ / 20 _____   junior

DATE _____ / _____ / 20 _____   senior

VIVIAN TENORIO

DATE   /   / 20   freshman

DATE   /   / 20   sophomore

DATE   /   / 20   junior

DATE   /   / 20   senior

DATE   /   / 20   freshman

DATE   /   / 20   sophomore

DATE   /   / 20   junior

DATE   /   / 20   senior

VIVIAN TENORIO

DATE   /   / 20   freshman

DATE   /   / 20   sophomore

DATE   /   / 20   junior

DATE   /   / 20   senior

DATE   /   / 20   freshman

DATE   /   / 20   sophomore

DATE   /   / 20   junior

DATE   /   / 20   senior

VIVIAN TENORIO

DATE   /   / 20   freshman

DATE   /   / 20   sophomore

DATE   /   / 20   junior

DATE   /   / 20   senior

DATE   /   / 20   freshman

DATE   /   / 20   sophomore

DATE   /   / 20   junior

DATE   /   / 20   senior

VIVIAN TENORIO

DATE   /   / 20   freshman

DATE   /   / 20   sophomore

DATE   /   / 20   junior

DATE   /   / 20   senior

DATE   /   / 20   freshman

DATE   /   / 20   sophomore

DATE   /   / 20   junior

DATE   /   / 20   senior

VIVIAN TENORIO

DATE   /   / 20   freshman

DATE   /   / 20   sophomore

DATE   /   / 20   junior

DATE   /   / 20   senior

DATE   /   / 20   freshman

DATE   /   / 20   sophomore

DATE   /   / 20   junior

DATE   /   / 20   senior

VIVIAN TENORIO

DATE   /   / 20   freshman

DATE   /   / 20   sophomore

DATE   /   / 20   junior

DATE   /   / 20   senior

DATE   /   / 20   freshman

DATE   /   / 20   sophomore

DATE   /   / 20   junior

DATE   /   / 20   senior

VIVIAN TENORIO

DATE   /   / 20   freshman

DATE   /   / 20   sophomore

DATE   /   / 20   junior

DATE   /   / 20   senior

DATE   /   / 20   freshman

DATE   /   / 20   sophomore

DATE   /   / 20   junior

DATE   /   / 20   senior

VIVIAN TENORIO

DATE   /   / 20   freshman

DATE   /   / 20   sophomore

DATE   /   / 20   junior

DATE   /   / 20   senior

DATE   /   / 20   freshman

DATE   /   / 20   sophomore

DATE   /   / 20   junior

DATE   /   / 20   senior

VIVIAN TENORIO

DATE   /   / 20   freshman

DATE   /   / 20   sophomore

DATE   /   / 20   junior

DATE   /   / 20   senior

DATE   /   / 20   freshman

DATE   /   / 20   sophomore

DATE   /   / 20   junior

DATE   /   / 20   senior

VIVIAN TENORIO

DATE   /   / 20   freshman

DATE   /   / 20   sophomore

DATE   /   / 20   junior

DATE   /   / 20   senior

DATE   /   / 20   freshman

DATE   /   / 20   sophomore

DATE   /   / 20   junior

DATE   /   / 20   senior

VIVIAN TENORIO

DATE   /   / 20   freshman

DATE   /   / 20   sophomore

DATE   /   / 20   junior

DATE   /   / 20   senior

DATE ____ / ____ / 20 ____   freshman

DATE ____ / ____ / 20 ____   sophomore

DATE ____ / ____ / 20 ____   junior

DATE ____ / ____ / 20 ____   senior

VIVIAN TENORIO

DATE   /   / 20   freshman

DATE   /   / 20   sophomore

DATE   /   / 20   junior

DATE   /   / 20   senior

DATE   /   / 20   freshman

DATE   /   / 20   sophomore

DATE   /   / 20   junior

DATE   /   / 20   senior

DATE   /   / 20   freshman

DATE   /   / 20   sophomore

DATE   /   / 20   junior

DATE   /   / 20   senior

DATE ___ / ___ / 20 ___   freshman

DATE ___ / ___ / 20 ___   sophomore

DATE ___ / ___ / 20 ___   junior

DATE ___ / ___ / 20 ___   senior

VIVIAN TENORIO

DATE   /   / 20   freshman

DATE   /   / 20   sophomore

DATE   /   / 20   junior

DATE   /   / 20   senior

DATE   /   / 20   freshman

DATE   /   / 20   sophomore

DATE   /   / 20   junior

DATE   /   / 20   senior

VIVIAN TENORIO

HOMECOMING Picture

DATE   /   /   LOVE?   ☐ Yes   ☐ No

DATE   /   / 20   freshman

DATE   /   / 20   sophomore

DATE   /   / 20   junior

DATE   /   / 20   senior

VIVIAN TENORIO

DATE　　/　　/ 20　　　　　　　　　　　　freshman

DATE　　/　　/ 20　　　　　　　　　　　　sophomore

DATE　　/　　/ 20　　　　　　　　　　　　junior

DATE　　/　　/ 20　　　　　　　　　　　　senior

DATE   /   / 20   freshman

DATE   /   / 20   sophomore

DATE   /   / 20   junior

DATE   /   / 20   senior

PROM Picture

PLACE PICTURE
HERE

DATE   /   /   LOVE? ☐ Yes   ☐ No

DATE   /   / 20   freshman

DATE   /   / 20   sophomore

DATE   /   / 20   junior

DATE   /   / 20   senior

VIVIAN TENORIO

DATE   /   / 20   freshman

DATE   /   / 20   sophomore

DATE   /   / 20   junior

DATE   /   / 20   senior

DATE   /   / 20   freshman

DATE   /   / 20   sophomore

DATE   /   / 20   junior

DATE   /   / 20   senior

DATE   /   / 20   freshman

DATE   /   / 20   sophomore

DATE   /   / 20   junior

DATE   /   / 20   senior

DATE   /   / 20   freshman

DATE   /   / 20   sophomore

DATE   /   / 20   junior

DATE   /   / 20   senior

VIVIAN TENORIO

DATE _____ / _____ / 20 _____   freshman

DATE _____ / _____ / 20 _____   sophomore

DATE _____ / _____ / 20 _____   junior

DATE _____ / _____ / 20 _____   senior

DATE   /   / 20   freshman

DATE   /   / 20   sophomore

DATE   /   / 20   junior

DATE   /   / 20   senior

VIVIAN TENORIO

DATE   /   / 20   freshman

DATE   /   / 20   sophomoro

DATE   /   / 20   junior

DATE   /   / 20   senior

DATE   /   / 20   freshman

DATE   /   / 20   sophomore

DATE   /   / 20   junior

DATE   /   / 20   senior

DATE   /   / 20   freshman

DATE   /   / 20   sophomore

DATE   /   / 20   junior

DATE   /   / 20   senior

DATE   /   / 20   freshman

DATE   /   / 20   sophomore

DATE   /   / 20   junior

DATE   /   / 20   senior

VIVIAN TENORIO

DATE   /   / 20   freshman

DATE   /   / 20   sophomoro

DATE   /   / 20   junior

DATE   /   / 20   senior

DATE   /   / 20   freshman

DATE   /   / 20   sophomore

DATE   /   / 20   junior

DATE   /   / 20   senior

SILLY Picture

PLACE PICTURE
HERE

DATE   /   /   LOVE?   ☐ Yes   ☐ No

DATE   /   / 20   freshman

DATE   /   / 20   sophomore

DATE   /   / 20   junior

DATE   /   / 20   senior

VIVIAN TENORIO

DATE   /   / 20   freshman

DATE   /   / 20   sophomore

DATE   /   / 20   junior

DATE   /   / 20   senior

DATE   /   / 20   freshman

DATE   /   / 20   sophomore

DATE   /   / 20   junior

DATE   /   / 20   senior

VIVIAN TENORIO

DATE   /   / 20   freshman

DATE   /   / 20   sophomore

DATE   /   / 20   junior

DATE   /   / 20   senior

DATE   /   / 20   freshman

DATE   /   / 20   sophomore

DATE   /   / 20   junior

DATE   /   / 20   senior

VIVIAN TENORIO

DATE _____ / _____ / 20 _____   freshman

DATE _____ / _____ / 20 _____   sophomore

DATE _____ / _____ / 20 _____   junior

DATE _____ / _____ / 20 _____   senior

DATE   /   / 20   freshman

DATE   /   / 20   sophomore

DATE   /   / 20   junior

DATE   /   / 20   senior

VIVIAN TENORIO

DATE   /   / 20   freshman

DATE   /   / 20   sophomore

DATE   /   / 20   junior

DATE   /   / 20   senior

DATE   /   / 20   freshman

DATE   /   / 20   sophomore

DATE   /   / 20   junior

DATE   /   / 20   senior

VIVIAN TENORIO

DATE   /   / 20   freshman

DATE   /   / 20   sophomore

DATE   /   / 20   junior

DATE   /   / 20   senior

DATE   /   / 20   freshman

DATE   /   / 20   sophomore

DATE   /   / 20   junior

DATE   /   / 20   senior

VIVIAN TENORIO

DATE   /   / 20   freshman

DATE   /   / 20   sophomore

DATE   /   / 20   junior

DATE   /   / 20   senior

DATE   /   / 20   freshman

DATE   /   / 20   sophomore

DATE   /   / 20   junior

DATE   /   / 20   senior

VIVIAN TENORIO

DATE   /   / 20   freshman

DATE   /   / 20   sophomore

DATE   /   / 20   junior

DATE   /   / 20   senior

DATE   /   / 20   freshman

DATE   /   / 20   sophomore

DATE   /   / 20   junior

DATE   /   / 20   senior

VIVIAN TENORIO

DATE   /   / 20   freshman

DATE   /   / 20   sophomore

DATE   /   / 20   junior

DATE   /   / 20   senior

DATE   /   / 20   freshman

DATE   /   / 20   sophomore

DATE   /   / 20   junior

DATE   /   / 20   senior

VIVIAN TENORIO

DATE   /   / 20   freshman

DATE   /   / 20   sophomore

DATE   /   / 20   junior

DATE   /   / 20   senior

DATE   /   / 20   freshman

DATE   /   / 20   sophomore

DATE   /   / 20   junior

DATE   /   / 20   senior

VIVIAN TENORIO

DATE   /   / 20   freshman

DATE   /   / 20   sophomore

DATE   /   / 20   junior

DATE   /   / 20   senior

HIGH SCHOOL JOURNAL

DATE   /   / 20   freshman

DATE   /   / 20   sophomore

DATE   /   / 20   junior

DATE   /   / 20   senior

VIVIAN TENORIO

DATE   /   / 20   freshman

DATE   /   / 20   sophomore

DATE   /   / 20   junior

DATE   /   / 20   senior

DATE   /   / 20   freshman

DATE   /   / 20   sophomore

DATE   /   / 20   junior

DATE   /   / 20   senior

VIVIAN TENORIO

DATE ___/___/ 20_____   freshman

DATE ___/___/ 20_____   sophomore

DATE ___/___/ 20_____   junior

DATE ___/___/ 20_____   senior

DATE   /   / 20   freshman

DATE   /   / 20   sophomore

DATE   /   / 20   junior

DATE   /   / 20   senior

VIVIAN TENORIO

DATE   /   / 20   freshman

DATE   /   / 20   sophomore

DATE   /   / 20   junior

DATE   /   / 20   senior

DATE   /   / 20   freshman

DATE   /   / 20   sophomore

DATE   /   / 20   junior

DATE   /   / 20   senior

DATE   /   / 20   freshman

DATE   /   / 20   sophomore

DATE   /   / 20   junior

DATE   /   / 20   senior

DATE   /   / 20   freshman

DATE   /   / 20   sophomore

DATE   /   / 20   junior

DATE   /   / 20   senior

VIVIAN TENORIO

DATE _____ / _____ / 20 _____   freshman

DATE _____ / _____ / 20 _____   sophomore

DATE _____ / _____ / 20 _____   junior

DATE _____ / _____ / 20 _____   senior

DATE   /   / 20   freshman

DATE   /   / 20   sophomore

DATE   /   / 20   junior

DATE   /   / 20   senior

VIVIAN TENORIO

DATE   /   / 20   freshman

DATE   /   / 20   sophomore

DATE   /   / 20   junior

DATE   /   / 20   senior

DATE   /   / 20   freshman

DATE   /   / 20   sophomore

DATE   /   / 20   junior

DATE   /   / 20   senior

VIVIAN TENORIO

DATE   /   / 20   freshman

DATE   /   / 20   sophomoro

DATE   /   / 20   junior

DATE   /   / 20   senior

DATE   /   / 20   freshman

DATE   /   / 20   sophomore

DATE   /   / 20   junior

DATE   /   / 20   senior

VIVIAN TENORIO

DATE   /   / 20   freshman

DATE   /   / 20   sophomore

DATE   /   / 20   junior

DATE   /   / 20   senior

DATE   /   / 20   freshman

DATE   /   / 20   sophomore

DATE   /   / 20   junior

DATE   /   / 20   senior

VIVIAN TENORIO

DATE   /   / 20   freshman

DATE   /   / 20   sophomore

DATE   /   / 20   junior

DATE   /   / 20   senior

DATE   /   / 20   freshman

DATE   /   / 20   sophomore

DATE   /   / 20   junior

DATE   /   / 20   senior

VIVIAN TENORIO

DATE   /   / 20   freshman

DATE   /   / 20   sophomore

DATE   /   / 20   junior

DATE   /   / 20   senior

DATE   /   / 20   freshman

DATE   /   / 20   sophomore

DATE   /   / 20   junior

DATE   /   / 20   senior

VIVIAN TENORIO

DATE   /   / 20   freshman

DATE   /   / 20   sophomore

DATE   /   / 20   junior

DATE   /   / 20   senior

DATE   /   / 20   freshman

DATE   /   / 20   sophomore

DATE   /   / 20   junior

DATE   /   / 20   senior

VIVIAN TENORIO

DATE   /   / 20   freshman

DATE   /   / 20   sophomore

DATE   /   / 20   junior

DATE   /   / 20   senior

DATE   /   / 20   freshman

DATE   /   / 20   sophomore

DATE   /   / 20   junior

DATE   /   / 20   senior

VIVIAN TENORIO

DATE   /   / 20   freshman

DATE   /   / 20   sophomore

DATE   /   / 20   junior

DATE   /   / 20   senior

DATE   /   / 20   freshman

DATE   /   / 20   sophomore

DATE   /   / 20   junior

DATE   /   / 20   senior

VIVIAN TENORIO

DATE   /   / 20   freshman

DATE   /   / 20   sophomore

DATE   /   / 20   junior

DATE   /   / 20   senior

DATE   /   / 20   freshman

DATE   /   / 20   sophomore

DATE   /   / 20   junior

DATE   /   / 20   senior

VIVIAN TENORIO

DATE _____ / _____ / 20 _____ freshman

DATE _____ / _____ / 20 _____ sophomore

DATE _____ / _____ / 20 _____ junior

DATE _____ / _____ / 20 _____ senior

DATE   /   / 20   freshman

DATE   /   / 20   sophomore

DATE   /   / 20   junior

DATE   /   / 20   senior

VIVIAN TENORIO

DATE   /   / 20   freshman

DATE   /   / 20   sophomore

DATE   /   / 20   junior

DATE   /   / 20   senior

DATE   /   / 20   freshman

DATE   /   / 20   sophomore

DATE   /   / 20   junior

DATE   /   / 20   senior

VIVIAN TENORIO

DATE   /   / 20   freshman

DATE   /   / 20   sophomore

DATE   /   / 20   junior

DATE   /   / 20   senior

DATE   /   / 20   freshman

DATE   /   / 20   sophomore

DATE   /   / 20   junior

DATE   /   / 20   senior

VIVIAN TENORIO

DATE   /   / 20   freshman

DATE   /   / 20   sophomore

DATE   /   / 20   junior

DATE   /   / 20   senior

DATE   /   / 20   freshman

DATE   /   / 20   sophomore

DATE   /   / 20   junior

DATE   /   / 20   senior

VIVIAN TENORIO

DATE   /   / 20   freshman

DATE   /   / 20   sophomore

DATE   /   / 20   junior

DATE   /   / 20   senior

best friends

PLACE PICTURE
HERE

DATE   /   /   LOVE?   ☐ Yes   ☐ No

VIVIAN TENORIO

DATE   /   / 20   freshman

DATE   /   / 20   sophomore

DATE   /   / 20   junior

DATE   /   / 20   senior

HIGH SCHOOL JOURNAL

DATE   /   / 20   freshman

DATE   /   / 20   sophomore

DATE   /   / 20   junior

DATE   /   / 20   senior

VIVIAN TENORIO

DATE   /   / 20   freshman

DATE   /   / 20   sophomore

DATE   /   / 20   junior

DATE   /   / 20   senior

HIGH SCHOOL JOURNAL

DATE   /   / 20   freshman

DATE   /   / 20   sophomore

DATE   /   / 20   junior

DATE   /   / 20   senior

VIVIAN TENORIO

DATE   /   / 20   freshman

DATE   /   / 20   sophomore

DATE   /   / 20   junior

DATE   /   / 20   senior

DATE   /   / 20   freshman

DATE   /   / 20   sophomore

DATE   /   / 20   junior

DATE   /   / 20   senior

VIVIAN TENORIO

DATE   /   / 20   freshman

DATE   /   / 20   sophomore

DATE   /   / 20   junior

DATE   /   / 20   senior

DATE   /   / 20   freshman

DATE   /   / 20   sophomore

DATE   /   / 20   junior

DATE   /   / 20   senior

VIVIAN TENORIO

DATE   /   / 20   freshman

DATE   /   / 20   sophomore

DATE   /   / 20   junior

DATE   /   / 20   senior

DATE   /   / 20   freshman

DATE   /   / 20   sophomore

DATE   /   / 20   junior

DATE   /   / 20   senior

VIVIAN TENORIO

DATE   /   / 20 _____ freshman

DATE   /   / 20 _____ sophomore

DATE   /   / 20 _____ junior

DATE   /   / 20 _____ senior

DATE   /   / 20   freshman

DATE   /   / 20   sophomore

DATE   /   / 20   junior

DATE   /   / 20   senior

VIVIAN TENORIO

DATE   /   / 20   freshman

DATE   /   / 20   sophomore

DATE   /   / 20   junior

DATE   /   / 20   senior

DATE   /   / 20   freshman

DATE   /   / 20   sophomore

DATE   /   / 20   junior

DATE   /   / 20   senior

VIVIAN TENORIO

DATE   /   / 20   freshman

DATE   /   / 20   sophomore

DATE   /   / 20   junior

DATE   /   / 20   senior

DATE   /   / 20   freshman

DATE   /   / 20   sophomore

DATE   /   / 20   junior

DATE   /   / 20   senior

VIVIAN TENORIO

DATE   /   / 20   freshman

DATE   /   / 20   sophomore

DATE   /   / 20   junior

DATE   /   / 20   senior

Best Day of...

my freshman year:

my sophomore year:

my junior year:

my senior year:

"What do you want to be when you grow up?"

Freshman Year:

Sophomore Year:

Junior Year:

Senior Year:

About the Author

Vivian's belief in thinking that anything was possible if she just put her mind to it helped her deal with and hustle through the challenges she faced as a teenage mother, young wife and high school dropout.

This no-limits attitude led her to open a restaurant, start Signature Flan, start a publishing company "JAV Publishing", and become the author of her 1st book and now creator of a series of journals.

Websites
www.viviantenorio.com
www.YouTube.com/SecretLifeofVivian

Made in United States
Orlando, FL
20 July 2022

19988098R00114